Imagi
James Robert

Contents

Chapter 1	*The Move*	5
Chapter 2	*The Trip*	9
Chapter 3	*The Hotel*	13
Chapter 4	*The Lesson*	20
Chapter 5	*The Coach*	25
Chapter 6	*The Deal*	30
Chapter 7	*The Plan*	36
Chapter 8	*The Price*	43
Chapter 9	*The Pay-off*	48
Chapter 10	*The End...?*	56

Chapter 1

The Move

He was smothering! He must escape, and quickly! Adam Quest finally pulled himself free from the clinging hands that held him back. He slowly staggered over to his caravan of camels, which awaited to take him on his odyssey across the barren desert. "Really, dear people, thank you for your warm regard, but now I must be off!" Quest cried as he seated himself on the lead camel. This was undoubtedly the part he hated most. No matter how well prepared he was for his adventures, no matter how he thirsted for new and exciting experiences, he always dreaded the goodbyes. Free from the adoring grasp of his well-wishers, he set off, turning back only to wave one last time...

"James Robert Howard! Wait a minute, you forgot your backpack!" called Mrs Watkins, as she bustled up behind him in the school hallway. "You ran out of the class so fast, I didn't get a chance to tell you how much we're all going to miss you. Please write to us and let us know how you like your new school."

Jim choked on the lump in his throat that he'd been fighting all day. He didn't want his teacher to see him behaving like a baby. No matter what he tried to imagine, nothing made it any better, and he was going to have to face facts. We're just moving, he told himself. People do it all the time.

"Thanks, Mrs Watkins. I'm going to miss you, too," Jim mumbled. "Well, I think Mum is probably waiting for me outside. I've got to go…" He turned and ran. If Mrs Watkins hugged him once more, he'd lose it completely.

Mum smiled kindly as he came up to the car. "How was your last day, Jim?" she asked. "It must have been pretty tough. It won't be so bad, and you can always invite your friends to come for a visit. They'd love the chance to stay for a while at a ski resort."

Jim nodded. They had been over it a hundred times. Ever since Mum had received the job offer to manage the main office of a big resort hotel, it was all his parents had talked about. He knew that Mum and Dad were excited about the chance to move to the mountains, but all it meant to him was that he was moving away from the only home he'd ever known. They wouldn't even be able to spend the next holidays at home. The hotel needed Mum to help them through an extremely important ski competition that was less than a week away.

The very fact that they were moving to a ski town made it even worse. I bet everybody there will know how to ski, Jim groaned to himself. I'll be the only one who doesn't, and I'll be totally left out. I'll never be able to make any new friends.

Jim sat on his rolled-up sleeping-bag in the middle of his empty room. The family had "camped" on its last night in the house because all of the furniture was already packed and gone. His room looked so different without his things in it. It really didn't belong to him any more.

"Jim, would you help me carry this last box out to the car?" Dad called. As they struggled with the box, Dad said, "You know, your mum and I really appreciate the way you've pitched in. I know it's hard to move, especially in the middle of the year, but you've been a great help. I'll have a couple of weeks before I begin my new editor's job and you won't be starting school again until a bit later so, perhaps, we could have a couple of weeks together, and you could start skiing!"

Jim just nodded. Skiing again. He wasn't even sure if he really *wanted* to know how to ski, but it was all his parents ever talked about these days. He tossed his sleeping-bag in the car and climbed in beside it. As they drove away, he turned around and watched until his old home disappeared from view.

Chapter 2

The Trip

The cold is a deceptive killer. It lulls you into exhaustion, never letting on you are its prisoner until it's too late. As Admiral Thor Osgood shook his head to clear the snow-blindness that had haunted him for most of his journey across the vast Arctic wasteland, chunks of ice fell from his heavy beard. Frozen to the core, he knew he was almost done in. His team of sled dogs was gone, attacked and eaten by a savage polar bear. With the few supplies left to him, he had continued on alone. Now he was pitted against a howling blizzard. He must keep moving. He must reach the town! If he allowed himself to rest out here in the open, he would never make it through the night...

"James Robert, where on earth is your coat? It's freezing out here!" Mum ran up to him with his coat and hat. "I know you just want to stretch your legs for a minute while we get petrol, but you can't be careless and let your imagination run away with you up here. You never know when the next storm might happen."

Jim quickly zipped up his coat. So, on top of everything else, killer blizzards can happen at a moment's notice. Normally, his parents just dragged him out into this hostile wilderness for holidays. Now he was going to have to *live* here. He trudged back to the car through the snow. Only a couple more hours of driving, then he'd see what he was really up against.

Once the family was on the road again, Dad handed him a magazine he'd bought at the petrol station. "Take a look at some of these pictures. If that doesn't get you excited about skiing, I don't know what will! The man on the cover is Steve Sanders, one of the country's best downhill racers. It says he started skiing when he was only a couple of years younger than you are."

But what a difference a couple of years can make, Jim sighed to himself. It just proves that everyone up there will have years more experience than I do. I'll never be able to catch up, even if I can do it at all.

To get his parents off the subject of skiing, Jim started to ask them questions about the town to which they were moving. His parents were pleased with his interest, and willingly described the wild, scenic mountains that surrounded the town. When it came to the town itself, however, the conversation stopped. Apart from their new jobs, his parents didn't know much about what the town had to offer. They didn't even know where they were going to live yet, so they were all going to stay at the hotel for the first month or so.

Mum turned to him a little anxiously. "I know how important the holidays are to you, Jim, and I hope you don't mind spending them in an hotel room."

Actually, Jim didn't really mind that part at all. Because his parents were so completely mad about camping, he'd never stayed in an hotel before, and it sounded like a lot of fun. "No problem, Mum. I think it'll be great to stay at the hotel. This will be the first time you've ever taken me to a place that has an actual swimming pool. What could be better than that?"

As his parents continued to discuss the hotel, Jim started to feel his first stirrings of interest. The hotel sounded absolutely huge, and Mum seemed a little nervous about working in such a large place.

"You'll be fine," Dad assured her. "You said yourself that Mr Bloom was great when he interviewed you."

"Yes, but I won't be working for him. I'll be working for the hotel manager, Mr Stadnick, and rumour has it that he is a real tyrant."

"Mum, if he gives you a hard time, just call the local newspaper, and I'll bet the new editor will put it on the front page. Won't you, Dad?" Everyone laughed, and Jim sat back, thinking that perhaps the move wouldn't be so bad after all.

Chapter 3

The Hotel

The massive doors swung open slowly, and he walked warily into the lobby of the ancient hotel. Ambassador Derek Goodkind had travelled all over the world, but never before had the stakes been this high. He was ready for any manner of surprise or intrigue. He had agreed to this meeting on the enemy's turf, hoping that a little shrewd diplomacy could stop the war before it even began. He must not allow his nervousness to show, or all would be lost. He turned to his faithful assistant and said, "We have important work to do here, my friend, but watch your back. The walls in this noble old place have ears." With that, he snapped his fingers at the staff, and instructed them to carry his bags to his suite...

"James Robert Howard! Where are your manners?" his mother hissed. "You just snapped your fingers at Mr Stadnick. Now pay attention and be polite!"

Jim froze. Arms crossed, the short man was rocking angrily back and forth on his stumpy, little feet, a sneer disfiguring his lumpy face. Jim's mum swallowed, then smiled hesitantly at her new boss. "I'm sorry, my son has a very active imagination, and sometimes it just runs away with him. I…"

"Well," barked Mr Stadnick, "just make sure he doesn't ever do that to one of our guests, or you will really have some explaining to do. So, you think you know your job, hmmm? Why don't you show me what you think you know. I have a stack of reservations for you to start processing."

"Mr Stadnick, it is already after seven, and we've been driving for the past ten hours. I'd really like to have a chance to settle in. I will, however, see you bright and early tomorrow morning," Jim's mum said, her chin held high.

"Oh, so that's how it is. I hope you aren't going to make a habit of this. You are here to work, not holiday. I suppose you know that you have one of our best rooms? Mr Bloom insisted, for some reason, even though I tried to convince him that we could easily fill it, especially during the Olympic trials. I just hope you're worth the trouble."

Mum gave Mr Stadnick a small, tight smile, and turned to get the key to the room. Jim could see that she was really upset, and was trying her hardest not to let it show. She grabbed Jim's arm, and rushed back out to the car, where Dad was waiting.

"Oh! That obnoxious man! I hope that was just a slip, because if he's like that all the time, this move could turn out to be a mistake," Jim's mum told his dad as they carried their bags down the hall to their room.

"Aw, don't worry about it. He's just trying to show you who's the boss. Once he sees how good you are, it won't matter."

"Oh, Mum, this isn't a mistake. It's going to be great! I'm really glad we've got the chance to live up here." Poor Mum! Jim told himself. I'm not going to let her know how much I hate this. She has enough to worry about as it is.

When the family entered the hotel room, they momentarily forgot about Mr Stadnick. No wonder this was supposed to be one of the hotel's best rooms; it was huge! A large fireplace dominated the sitting area, which separated the suite's two bedrooms. Jim had never expected anything this nice, and he certainly had not expected to have a room of his own.

"There, you see, honey?" Dad said. "Mr Bloom insisted we have this room, so he must be pretty impressed with you. And, remember, he owns the hotel. Everything is going to be fine."

I hope so, thought Jim. After seeing Mr Stadnick in person, he wasn't so sure.

The next morning, Jim's mum had already gone when he and his dad got up. She'd left a note telling them where the dining-room was so they could get some breakfast. There were also, Jim realized with a groan, instructions on how to get to the ski area.

"This is going to be fun!" Dad exclaimed. "It looks like your mum won't have much free time to look for a house yet, so we might as well get you started on your pro skiing career straight away. After breakfast, we'll hire some equipment for you."

Jim dawdled as much as he possibly could, but eventually he was ready to go. As he went out to meet Dad, he passed through the lobby, where he caught sight of his mum rushing around in the back office. He waved to her.

"Excuse me, are you Mrs Howard's son?" Jim turned to see a cheerful blonde receptionist standing behind the front desk. "My name is Robyn. Welcome to Ski Inn! We're all so glad that your mum is finally here. She seems really nice. Too bad she had to start on such an awful day."

Jim introduced himself, and then asked, "What do you mean, such an awful day? What's going on?"

"Oh, you haven't heard yet? I thought that with all the shouting, the entire town must know by now. Apparently, the skier Steve Sanders – you know, the Olympic hopeful – had reservations to stay here with his coach during the trials, but we couldn't find any reservations for them on our computer. The hotel is full, and Mr Stadnick wanted your mum to

give up your room for them to use," Robyn said, without taking so much as a breath.

"Oh, no!" Jim breathed. "You know, he said last night that he didn't like us staying here. No wonder, if the hotel is full! Do we need to start packing now?" Although that would be a hassle, Jim knew it would at least postpone the skiing.

"No, I think everything is OK now. At first, Mr Stadnick was bellowing his head off, and Mr Ratner – that's Steve's coach – was shouting, and everybody was in trouble," Robyn said. She leaned over the front desk and added more quietly, "Luckily, your mum solved the problem. She found a big mistake that Mr Stadnick had made on the computer and discovered that we really had more rooms than we thought. Gee, that *really* pushed him over the edge!"

So Mum had bagged a victory. Good. Jim was ready to start asking Robyn for more details when he caught sight of his dad waving at him impatiently. "It was nice meeting you, Robyn. That's my dad out there. He wants to take me skiing," Jim said in a doom-laden voice.

"Skiing? Don't worry, you'll love it," Robyn said. "I started to ski when I was just about your age, and it's my favourite thing in the whole world. You'll be great!"

"Great?" Jim murmured as he plodded out of the lobby. "I just hope I get back alive."

Chapter 4

The Lesson

The pressure was on. It all came down to this. Years of training were on the line, an immeasurable sacrifice of time and youth. Ace Avalanche's eyes swept over the hordes of cheering people. He gave himself a shake, and thought; my team-mate cracked his head after crashing on the third turn, I'm our only hope. I must beat the world-record time set by the ruthless Swede, Lars Stumblum, and bring home a gold medal for my country. Ace nodded to the starter, "Ready when you are." He crouched down, muscles coiled like a tiger ready to spring. At the sound of the gun, he leapt forward to attack the steep and treacherous course…

"James Robert, look out!" shouted Dad, as Jim slid into the back of the ski-lift queue. "I'm sorry, I'm sorry," Jim's dad stammered to the people who were tangled in a heap on top of Jim. "It's his very first time on skis…"

Jim pulled himself with difficulty from the pile, and smiled sheepishly. "How do you stop on these things?"

"Well, really," muttered an angry woman as she pulled herself up. "I didn't come all this way to rough-house with hooligans! You ridiculous amateurs are dangerous – running amuck and barrelling into innocent bystanders. If you don't know what you're doing, take a lesson!"

Jim's dad swallowed, apologized again, and turned to Jim. "You know, slugger, that's really not such a bad idea. Perhaps a real ski lesson would help you more than I can. It's been a long time since I've done this, myself."

With that, he grabbed Jim's shoulders and steered him across the snow towards some other kids, who were lining up behind a ski instructor. Before Jim could even protest, he was signed up, and Dad was waving goodbye. As he watched Dad clomp away, someone clapped him on the back, knocking him off his feet, again.

"Whoa, there, young fellow! You seem to be a bit shaky on your stems, now, don't you?" boomed the ski instructor. She was a tall, sturdy woman, with a red face, and a long, blonde braid stretching down her back. "Well, we'll take care of that in no time. Since you seem to be the oldest, you can lead the group up to the chair-lift."

The oldest? Jim looked around. Sure enough, he was at least three years older than every other kid in the group. Oh great, he thought, can it get any worse than this? Resigned to a terrible morning, Jim shuffled off to the ski-lift queue.

While they waited, the instructor called out instructions on how to get on and off the lift, and

Jim tried to memorize every word. A five-year-old girl was waiting in the queue next to him and, when it was their turn to get on the chair, he would have missed entirely if she hadn't helped him. Jim was so humiliated that when the time came to get off, he wasn't paying attention, and the tip of his ski caught, flipping him face down into the snow. The lift operator reached over and pulled him out of the way. "Hey, kid, watch what you're doing!" the operator shouted. Gritting his teeth, Jim struggled upright yet again.

While Jim tried to get himself together, the instructor began teaching the rest of the class how to snowplough down the bunny slope. "Well, now, it's a piece of cake, isn't it, gang? Just point the tips of your skis together, and you slow down. See?" The class followed behind her, imitating her perfectly.

That is, everyone but Jim. He started to slide, and soon he was totally out of control again. He tried to snowplough, but the tips of his skis crossed, and he started to slide sideways down the mountain, picking up speed as he went. Poles flailing, he crashed into a bush at the side of the run.

"Wow, what a wipe-out!" guffawed the ski instructor. "How about a hand getting out of that bush? That's the best crash I've seen in a long time!"

Jim was totally winded, and he felt as though even his bruises had bruises. One of his skis had slid down to the bottom of the hill, and one of his poles was bent. "I think I've really hurt my leg," he said, doubtfully. "I don't think I should ski any more…"

"Rubbish!" said the ski instructor. "That bush just broke your fall. Let's get your ski and try again. You'll get it, I promise."

"No, I really think I did something to my leg," Jim insisted. "I don't want to risk making it even worse. I'll just go down and wait for Dad."

The instructor just shook her head and radioed to one of her fellow instructors, who came up to take over the class. She then skied Jim down the rest of the bunny slope, guiding him on his one ski between her two. At the bottom, Jim muttered an embarrassed thank you. He shoved all of his ski equipment in the locker Dad had rented, then limped over to a bench to wait.

The whole experience had been worse than anything he could have ever imagined, which was really saying something.

Chapter 5

The Coach

The pain was wretched. His breath hissed between clenched teeth as he shifted his weight to relieve the pressure on his wounded leg. The accident had been gruesome, but officer Cameron Valiant knew his heroic sacrifice had been worth it. When he had seen the car hurtling towards the shoppers, he hadn't thought twice. He threw himself in the path of the automobile, pushing the innocent bystanders out of harm's way, and taking the full impact himself. Now, if only he could just get through the next few torturous hours, his shattered body would begin to knit together, and his outraged nerve endings would relax their vicious onslaught. He would face the pain as he faced every challenge – courageously…

"James Robert," sighed Dad, "do you really expect me to believe that your absolute refusal to ski any more is a noble gesture to save humanity?"

"Dad, I'm dangerous on skis. You heard that woman in the lift queue. Then I had to crash so I wouldn't run over one of those little kids in my class, and it practically broke my leg!"

"Jim, your instructor said you slid into a bush. It happens to all beginner skiers, so don't feel too badly about it." He lifted up the ice-pack that Jim had put on his knee. "Your leg isn't swollen. I think you just have sore muscles. If it's any consolation, I do, too."

"Dad, I just think I really should rest it for a couple of days, just to make sure…" Jim felt a little sheepish. His leg *was* feeling a little better but, perhaps, that was because of the ice-pack. He swallowed. "You always say it's far better to be safe than sorry."

Dad turned and walked away. Jim knew his dad was disappointed, but facing his father's disappointment seemed easier than facing another trip up the mountain.

"You idiot! You clumsy, lazy, weak idiot!" a man's angry voice thundered through the lobby of the hotel, where Jim was lounging. Jim swivelled his head around. Who, in the world, was that?

"Why do I bother wasting my time with you? I could be coaching someone good, someone like Grant Grodecky. I thought you had talent and potential. The way you're performing, you couldn't ski your way out of a wet paper bag!"

"I'm sorry, Coach Ratner," said the flustered young athlete. "I just don't know what's happening to me up there."

Jim couldn't believe his eyes. There, right in front of him, stood Steve Sanders, the champion skier he'd read about in the magazine Dad had given him. But it didn't sound as if his skiing was any more successful than Jim's!

"I don't want to hear any more of your pathetic excuses," growled the red-faced Coach Ratner. He started to mimic Steve. "'My ski binding felt loose.' 'My helmet came undone.' 'I didn't hear your instructions.' If I hadn't signed a contract to coach you through these trials, I would have resigned months ago."

"Excuse me, Mr Ratner?" Mum walked up and beamed her most charming smile. "I've left several messages for you, but I suppose you haven't had a chance to speak to me yet. Now, I know how busy you are, but may I ask how you'll be paying your bill?"

"How dare you interrupt me? I'm right in the middle of something very important with Steve Sanders…" Coach Ratner spluttered, gesturing to where Steve had been standing only a few moments before. "Where is he? Where did he go? There, do you see what you've done? I was coaching this boy, and because of *your* interruption, he might not know what he needs to know in order to win his next race. And if he doesn't win his next race, he won't make it to the Olympics. Are you satisfied?" he bellowed.

Jim's mum paused, took a deep breath, and was steeling herself to continue, when Mr Stadnick came waddling up. "Mrs Howard, what is the meaning of this? You're upsetting one of our most important guests! Mr Ratner, what's going on?"

"Well," spluttered the coach, "I was giving Steve Sanders some important skiing tips, and this lackey of yours barged in and practically accused me of being a thief!"

"Why, Mrs Howard, I'm surprised at you. Wait for me in my office," the manager said self-importantly. He puffed out his chest even further, and smiled at the coach. "Mr Ratner, allow me to apologize on behalf of the Ski Inn. I assure you I will take care of everything, personally."

As Mr Stadnick followed Jim's mum into the office, Jim overheard her say, "I didn't call that man a thief. The cheques he writes keep bouncing, and his credit card has been cancelled. He's been running up bills for hundreds of dollars, and this hotel can't afford to lose any money if he walks out without paying us."

"Mrs Howard, I convinced Mr Ratner to stay in our hotel, and I will vouch for him myself. And if you continue trying to drive guests out of our hotel by calling them such rude names, I'll tell Mr Bloom that *you* are the reason we've been losing money," he blustered.

Jim couldn't believe what he was hearing. He was so irate that he almost missed seeing Mr Stadnick look back and wink at Coach Ratner, whose sharp, red face was contorted with waves of sniggering laughter.

Chapter 6

The Deal

As he closed in on his elusive quarry, secret agent Lance Valour knew his latest assignment had just taken another extremely ugly turn. His prey was none other than Sinister Samson, a cruel con man who had begun his long career in crime by robbing his own grandmother. To make matters even worse, Samson was on his way to a secret meeting with Moneybags Mack. If a plan were backed by Mack's money and Samson's brains, there would be no telling how much horrible pain and suffering the despicable duo might cause. Despite the risk of blowing his painstakingly created cover, agent Valour knew he had to get close enough to hear the two men's evil scheme. Then, no matter how, no matter what, he would have to risk everything to stop them…

"James Robert! What are you doing over here? I thought you'd hurt your leg and couldn't move."

Robyn. Of all the rotten luck! Just when he was trying to follow Coach Ratner through the ski area. The coach had shouted at Mum in the hotel lobby again, then suddenly broken off, saying he had an important meeting. Jim was convinced that Coach Ratner and Mr Stadnick were up to something, and he was dying to see if he could find out what it was. "Uh, hello, Robyn. I hardly recognized you away from the front desk," Jim said. "Is today your day off or something?"

"Yes, I thought I'd come up here to try to watch some of the ski races. It isn't every day that we have world-class skiers competing here. I think I blew it, though. You can't see anything from here. No wonder it's so deserted!"

"I think everyone's over on the other side of the lift. I'm supposed to meet Dad there in twenty minutes. You'd have to hurry to get a good spot, but it'd probably be worth it..." Jim said. Robyn was friendly, but just now he really couldn't stay to talk. Coach Ratner was almost out of sight! Jim started to edge away.

"Hey, you're not limping any more. Congratulations! No wonder you're out here in the fresh air. Is it getting you in the mood for your next lesson?" Robyn asked. Apparently, she wanted to chat more than she wanted to see the skiers, and Jim was starting to feel a bit desperate.

"Yeah, that's right, skiing. Look, I'm sorry, but I *really* have to go. See you later!" Jim took off at a run after the coach, who had just disappeared around a building.

In his hurry, Jim shot around the corner and almost ran right into Coach Ratner, who was deep in whispered conversation with a tall, heavy-set man dressed in a shiny suit and lots of tacky jewellery. The two men were standing in front of Grodecky's Grotto, which Jim had heard was the most popular restaurant in town. It was owned by the father of Steve Sander's arch-rival, Grant Grodecky.

Coach Ratner turned to look at Jim. "Stupid kids," he muttered to the tall man. "Come on, Grodecky. This pavement is like a railway station, and I don't really want anyone to see me with you in front of your place." They ducked into the restaurant.

Jim's initial disappointment that he hadn't caught Coach Ratner talking to Mr Stadnick faded. The coach seemed to be involved in all sorts of strange things, Jim thought to himself, and Grodecky seemed to be part of it all. Jim walked around to the alley behind the restaurant. He had a vague idea about looking through the rubbish, to see if he could find out anything.

His idea about searching through the rubbish seemed a lot less appealing after Jim peeked into the large, filthy bin. All of the restaurant's rubbish was in there, and it certainly looked revolting. Still, he didn't have any better ideas, so he hoisted himself up to get a better look, slipped on some of the grease dripping down the sides, and fell straight in.

"Gross!" groaned Jim, as he struggled to right himself. He was just getting ready to climb out when the back door of the restaurant opened. Mr Grodecky peeked out.

"Coast is clear," he said, and Coach Ratner joined him in front of the rubbish bin.

Jim couldn't believe his luck. Holding his breath to try to block out the stench of the rotting food, he listened intently.

"So, what's the big hold-up, Ratner?" Mr Grodecky growled. "I'm telling you, if I don't see better results and soon, you can just kiss that money I was going to give you goodbye."

"Hey, I'm doing my best. That Sanders kid is a good skier. If I'm too obvious, people might notice, and then the plan would be ruined. But I'm happy to say that his confidence is completely shot, and his performance times stink almost as much as all this rubbish. Your son won't have any trouble beating him in these trials."

"Well, you just better be sure that's the way it happens. There's room for only one more person on the Olympic team, and my son, Grant, better be the one," Grodecky said. "Remember, once Sanders is out of contention for the team, your contract with him is cancelled, and you can come to work for me, officially."

Coach Ratner laughed his horrible, sniggering laugh. "At the rate Sanders is fading, this might kill his career altogether. I'll have him so shattered that he'll take up knitting instead."

Mr Grodecky clapped him on the back. "You do that, and I'll double your payment. Let's get back inside. It's freezing out here."

As the two men walked back inside, Jim eased out of the rubbish bin. He was covered with crusty tomato sauce and revolting slime, and he knew his mum would go berserk when she saw how filthy he was. But, he reflected, it had been well worth it.

Chapter 7

The Plan

A savage snarl tore through the still air, a blood-chilling warning that signalled danger in any language. With lightning-fast reflexes, world-renowned lion tamer Dazzling Dave whirled and, with a loud crack of his whip, sent the enraged tiger charging back to his stand. Surrounded by a dozen of nature's fastest, shrewdest killers, Dazzling Dave knew his success depended on knowing and controlling where each cat was at every moment. As he stuck his head between the terrifically sharp teeth of a large lion, Dave prompted a sleek puma to leap through a blazing ring of fire. The audience gasped and Dave, every nerve-ending tuned to the cats, continued the work he loved best...

James Robert, he won't bite your head off. Just talk to him, Jim told himself. He had to speak to Steve Sanders while the champion skier was sitting here, alone, in the lodge.

"Mr S-s-s-an-n-ders," he stuttered. "I, uh, I'm James Robert… I mean, can I…"

"You want an autograph, kid? Well, here you are, but could you please leave me alone? I'm very busy right now," Steve muttered, pushing a hastily scrawled signature at Jim, then collapsing back into the sofa cushions and staring at the flames leaping in the fireplace.

Jim was going to have to do better than that. "Look, it's about your coach," he blurted. "He's trying to…"

"Yeah, he's trying to make a skier out of a nobody like me, right? Look, kid, leave me alone." Steve dragged himself off the couch and out of the front door, turning his back on Jim.

"Hey, James Robert, come over here." It was Robyn, at the front desk. "Don't feel too bad. Steve doesn't want to talk to anybody right now. He's in a real slump."

"But I need to tell him something important about his coach."

"That horrible Mr Ratner? I'd stay away from him if I were you." Robyn's face clouded. "Every time he walks through the front door, he has some complaint, and he keeps getting your mum into trouble. I've got to get that man off her back."

While they talked, an idea began to take shape in Jim's mind. "Hey, Robyn, I know a way you could take some of the wind out of the coach's sails, if you wouldn't mind keeping him here for a little while," he said. "What time is the semifinal race today?"

"In about two hours. Why?" Robyn asked.

"Well, when you see Coach Ratner leaving for the ski area, try to delay him. He *has* to miss the race today. It's important."

"Oh, I can certainly do that! I'll just put all of the hotel's phone calls on his bill, then ask him to sort out which calls are his. Believe me, it'll take forever! But I have to tell you, I don't see how this is going to help. Won't it just make him even meaner?"

Jim smiled mysteriously. "Just trust me, and I'll fill you in when I get a chance."

Having isolated the most dangerous lion, Jim rushed out of the door to deal with the rest.

❄

Some ski coaches were clustered together at the bottom of the hill, waiting for the race to begin. They were discussing the slumped form of Steve Sanders, who was hopelessly waiting nearby.

"That poor kid. Look at him over there. He's just about had it. It breaks my heart!"

"Yeah, if he doesn't hit his stride today, he's had it."

"I really thought he was going to be our man in this year's Olympics."

Jim smiled. If these other coaches were this sympathetic to Steve's troubles, his plan might work. Jim quickly scrawled a few words on the scrap of paper he was clutching, then approached the huddle.

"Excuse me. I have a message for you from Steve Sanders," he said, handing the paper to the coach who had spoken first.

The coach frowned and read the paper. "What's this about? Why would Steve want my help? Where's his coach?"

"I guess Coach Ratner had something else to do today," Jim said, smiling innocently. "He's a busy guy."

"Busy, my foot!" the coach exploded. "Deserting that poor kid on a day like today. That man's a rat. Well, that's Steve's signature, I'd recognize it anywhere. You bet I'll help him. Hey, Steve, Coach Smith to the rescue!" he called out, marching purposefully over to the skier, with Jim following at a run.

Steve looked puzzled, but Jim burst in before he could give the game away. "This coach just heard Coach Ratner can't make it. He said he'd be more than happy to give you some pointers for your run today."

Stunned, Steve said, "But…"

"Just don't say another word about it, son, I'm honoured!" Coach Smith boomed. "Let's take a last look at your equipment, and make sure everything is tight and tidy. All of this gear is going to have to be set just right for you to make it through the slalom at mid-mountain."

Jim moved away, hoping against hope that Robyn could keep Coach Ratner busy at the hotel long enough.

While Jim watched, he saw the new coach earnestly encouraging Steve, and Steve's chin start to rise as he felt the coach's confidence in him. Jim breathed a sigh of relief as he watched Steve head up to the top of the mountain with the last group of skiers. At least for the time being, he was out of Coach Ratner's grasp.

In fact, Coach Ratner arrived just as the final heat began. He ran up as Steve and the other competitor launched out of the starting gate and began their long, rapid descent of the mountain.

The two men swooped down the mountain, neck and neck. Jim didn't know much about skiing, but from listening to the sound of the crowd, he could tell the racers were closely matched. Then there was a gasp. Steve had misjudged one of the turns and almost gone down. The other skier was ahead. Jim didn't breathe as he watched Steve tuck even further and bullet down the hill, trying to save the race. It was going to be close.

Right at the finish line Steve's champion instincts prevailed, and he surged across the line, just ahead of the other racer. He had won the heat, but his error had cost him valuable time. His overall time was fourth fastest. It was not enough to guarantee him the Olympic slot, but good enough to get him into the finals the following day.

Jim leapt in the air. His plan had worked! He was so thrilled that it took him a minute to notice that an absolutely livid Mr Grodecky had stalked over to Coach Ratner, who was muttering frantically to him. The roar of the crowd prevented Jim from hearing what they were saying, but he could tell they were plotting something. He was horrified as he watched the coach smile viciously and mimic the action of snapping something in two.

Before, Coach Ratner had been satisfied with just stopping Steve by breaking his confidence. Now it looked as if he were willing to try breaking something else in order to get his money.

And it was up to Jim to stop him.

Chapter 8

The Price

It was so late. He pressed his index fingers against his tired eyes. Night had fallen many hours ago, and still the work continued. Trail-blazing research scientist Dr Rex Able was utterly exhausted, but he forced himself to lean over the microscope yet again. He was so close! He knew he was on the right track! He knew he was on the verge of isolating the devastating disease that was destroying the health of so many people. For years, doctors had believed that their patients were suffering from a myriad of different illnesses, but Dr Able had guessed that all of these sicknesses were rooted in a common malady. Now, if he could just prove the connection...

"James Robert, please pay attention!" Jim's mum sounded almost hysterical. "We're trying to have a family conference, and I'd appreciate it if you actually contributed something valuable instead of just sitting there, day-dreaming."

"Sorry, Mum," Jim mumbled.

Mum was upset following a terrible meeting she had had with Mr Stadnick. Jim, full of the events that had just happened at the ski slope, had walked into the lobby during the middle of it. Robyn, whose eyes were red from crying, went rushing past him as he entered.

Jim saw Mum and Mr Stadnick arguing in the office. Jim could overhear most of what was being said, and it didn't look good for either Mum or for Robyn.

"Mr Ratner is very upset, and so am I!" Mr Stadnick roared. "Do you realize what that ridiculous receptionist of yours did? She made him miss a very important race today!"

"If you're speaking of Robyn," Jim's mum said, fighting to keep her voice level, "she is the best receptionist we have, and I'm sure it was only a misunderstanding. You have no right to shout at her like that, especially in front of a guest."

"I have no right?" Mr Stadnick spluttered. "From what Mr Ratner tells me, you are just as incompetent as she is, and as soon as I have proof, I will see to it that you are both sacked. We don't need you here, no matter what Mr Bloom says, and I'm going to prove it to him!"

Jim's mum, white with fury, turned away and started to work at one of the computers. Mr Stadnick stalked back to his office, where someone was waiting for him. Jim felt no surprise whatsoever when he recognized Coach Ratner, who had a broad smile on his face.

As Mr Stadnick turned to shut his office door, Jim was horrified to see that he also wore a smug smile of satisfaction on his lumpy, little face. He was loving every minute of this! And, obviously, so was Coach Ratner. Briefly, Jim wondered whether Coach Ratner was involved in everything disagreeable that was going on in town.

And now, later that same evening, Jim and his parents sat having a family meeting. Mum was devastated, and the family was trying to work out its options.

"We gave up everything to come here," Mum said in a voice so low with despair that it sounded like a moan. "The house, our jobs, your school, and for what? It looks like I'm going to lose this job so fast I might as well never have had it."

"Darling, calm down," Jim's dad said kindly. "Until you hear something, anything, from Mr Bloom, your job is safe. No matter what happens, we'll make it through."

"Well, Mum," Jim added. "Everybody around here knows that Mr Stadnick is a fool. It's probably just his normal, everyday behaviour, and nothing more will come of it."

Although Jim said it to try to cheer up his mum, he doubted every word of it. Mr Stadnick was obviously plotting something with Coach Ratner, and now Jim's plan to help Steve had just given the two men more ammunition against Mum. Even worse, he had got Robyn, his only friend in the new town, into trouble as well.

As his parents continued talking, Jim felt his determination against Coach Ratner harden into steely resolve. Now that the futures of Steve, Robyn, and Mum depended on it, his job was more important than ever. Jim promised himself he would do everything in his power to stop the coach and his unscrupulous schemes. Everything!

Chapter 9

The Pay-off

It was too great a strain! The crippled plane screamed through the sky, every seam ready to burst from the force of the dive. Fighter pilot Stretch Baron fought to keep control. He had managed to evade an entire enemy squad, but one ruthless foe had managed to squeeze in a last, lucky shot. Stretch knew his time was running out. With no thought to his own safety, he used every last ounce of his brute strength to aim the crippled jet straight at a strategic bridge. If he could only hit it, the enemy would lose its only route to invade. Ignoring the danger, Baron stayed with the plane until he could be sure of his target. 2,000 feet... 1,000 feet... 500 feet. He had it! He ejected...

James Robert, you've got it! Jim was exultant. He had to get to Steve, and he had to do it fast. And now he knew how to do it. His wild imagination had actually come up with a solution!

It was all because his persistence had paid off. After a futile day of following Coach Ratner around the hotel, Jim had decided to strike up a conversation with the housekeeper who was just about to clean the coach's room. Under the pretence of helping her carry the vacuum cleaner into the room, Jim had seen exactly what the cruel coach was planning to do.

Although the coach had hurriedly gathered together his tools, Jim had caught a glimpse of a metal file and some tiny screws. The coach had been filing down the screws on Steve's bindings! The metal shavings scattered all over the bed proved it. With the high speeds and tight corners Steve would be facing on the mountain, there was no way that these skis would hold together. Steve was in real danger.

Jim knew if he said something to Coach Ratner now, the coach would just think of some other way to mess up the race. Jim simply had to get to the mountain to warn Steve himself.

❄

Jim stared at the crowds teeming in front of him. Steve was already waiting down at the bottom of the lift with the other finalists for the race to begin.

Jim knew he'd never be able to press through the crowds fast enough, let alone get close enough to warn Steve. If only he could cross the open expanse of snow below the finish line. But the race officials would nab him if they caught him trying to lumber through the deep snow.

"Unless," Jim said under his breath, "they *can't* catch me…" He was thinking about his skis, which were still in Dad's locker. He remembered the speed with which they had carried him over the snow. It just might work. Fear forgotten, he raced over and struggled to get himself into his equipment.

As Jim hurtled across the snow towards the skiers, he saw official after official gawk at his speeding form, then they remembered themselves and scrambled after him. "Help! I can't stop!" he shrieked. Arms flailing, he desperately tried to steer himself close enough.

I may not know how to ski, Jim muttered to himself, but I sure know how to crash. And crash he did, spectacularly, right in front of the skiers. "Steve! Steve!" he yelped, as the race officials closed in on him.

"Hey, Sanders, this kid wants to talk to you!" a large, sneering skier called. "Perhaps he wants some tips on how to wipe-out better. After all, you *are* the expert."

"Aw, cool it, Grant. Oh, it's *you* again. What on earth do you want, kid?" Steve said, suppressing a chuckle.

"Steve," Jim gasped. "Check your bindings. They're loose."

"What are you talking about? I raced on them yesterday, and they were just fine." Steve started to move away.

"No! Please! Steve, just look at them!" The race officials were trying to haul Jim away, and he was desperate. "Check the screws! Check the screws!" he shrieked as he was carried off.

Standing behind the rope which was holding back the spectators, Jim couldn't tell what was happening. Would Steve listen to him? Jim kept craning his neck to try to see what the skiers were doing, as the angry officials berated him.

"What are you doing, crashing into the skiers like that?"

"Where are your parents?"

"You rotten kid. Don't you think we have enough to worry about without you trying to ruin our security?"

"I'm really sorry, I'm just a beginner," Jim said absent-mindedly. The crowd was murmuring something. What was going on?

"Ladies and gentlemen. We've had a slight delay. The race will be postponed for fifteen minutes," the loudspeaker blared above Jim's head. Through the crowd, Jim saw Steve walking away from the other racers, carrying his skis. Jim slumped with relief. Steve had listened!

❄

The race was on. The tide of misfortune had turned. Luck had been on his side when he found out about his bindings, and now world-class skier Steve Sanders felt it would stay with him for the race. It was all up to him. He was on new, untested equipment for the biggest race of his life. He shook his head to clear the cobwebs of intruding doubts and fears. Luck was on his side. He was determined to win...

BANG! He was off! The falling snow whipped past his goggles, and the wind roared in his ears. He didn't even see the other skier schussing down the hill beside him. There was only the mountain, its path twisting and turning in front of him. He sheered by the first flag, its banner only millimetres from his face. He was cutting it close, but he had to. The second flag passed, then the third. He was like a machine. He didn't feel the cold. He didn't hear the crowd. The fourth and the fifth flags whipped past him. A rise in the hill. He soared over, moving faster than he'd ever moved in his life. He was ahead! He just had to win. He just had to!

There it was! He saw the finish line only as he was crossing it. Fighting the adrenalin, he forced his body to stop. He was down. He had no idea what his time was. He didn't care. He had done it! He had won! His crippling self-doubt was gone!

The loudspeaker blared out his time. He had broken the world record! His place in the Olympic team was all but assured. The crowd broke through the cordon and surged around him. As Steve tried to focus on the congratulations that were raining down on him, he noticed out of the corner of his eye a small figure standing quietly off to the side, smiling quietly. It was that strange kid again. How had he known about the bindings? Steve started to struggle through the crowd. What had the kid said his name was? Oh, yes...

"James Robert, could you come over here?" Steve called from the crowd of well-wishers that engulfed him.

Jim smiled, and started to walk over to Steve, skirting around Coach Ratner, who was desperately trying to fend off Mr Grodecky's pummelling fists and the whooshing ski poles of Grodecky's angry son, Grant.

Chapter 10

The End...?

A brilliant starburst flashed in front of him, then another and another. The crowd pressed ever closer. Voices demanded his attention. "Ladies and gentlemen, please, I'll just have to answer your questions one at a time." The hero smiled indulgently as he began his stalwart story of courageous conduct. The crowd "oohed" and "ahed" at each twist of his epic tale. After the struggle, the intrigue, and the danger, taming this gaggle of reporters and well-wishers seemed almost like child's play. "And that's how it happened," he concluded, to gasps of awe and wonderment. "I'm sure that any one of you would've done exactly the same..."

"James Robert, I think those skis suit you. Of course, you'll have to grow into them," Steve Sanders said. Jim had just finished telling his story to the small crowd that had gathered in the hotel lobby later that evening.

Jim blushed and glanced at the set of skis and poles that leaned against the wall next to him. Steve had insisted, saying that Jim deserved them, as he had saved the race. "Those are world-record skis," Steve said. Jim had never felt so proud.

"Well, slugger, that's quite a story," Dad said. "It looks like I'm going to have to start at the paper a couple of weeks early just to cover all of the news you've been stirring up. And I thought we were moving to a sleepy little town!"

"Dad and I were wondering where you'd been keeping yourself the past couple of days," Jim's mum added. "I thought you were avoiding us because you were afraid of skiing. We had no idea you were out fighting crime and corruption!"

"What's this about being afraid of skiing?" Steve asked. "The way you came shooting across the snow today, nobody would ever guess you were afraid of anything. You have the speed part down, now all you need is a little finesse. What about going skiing tomorrow and I'll show you a few things?"

Jim swallowed. Steve Sanders, champion skier, wanted to teach him how to ski? Before he could think of anything to say, Robyn burst out from the front desk. "Hey, James Robert! What's all this about you being a hero? Does this have anything to do with me getting into trouble for keeping Mr Ratner here before the race yesterday?"

"Oh, wow, Robyn, I'm sorry! I didn't want you to get into trouble, but you really saved the day. That coach was a rat, and you stopped him messing up Steve's race."

"Oh, she did, did she? How did she manage that?" said a deep voice behind the group.

"Daddy!" Robyn cried. "What are you doing up here?"

"Mr Bloom!" Jim's mum said at the very same instant.

Before the hotel's owner could explain, Mr Stadnick came waddling up.

"Mrs Howard! Robyn! Why aren't you two working? First you upset Mr Ratner, our most important guest, and now this. I've had enough of your incompetence, you lazy good-for-nothings!" he blustered. Then, turning to Mr Bloom, he said in his sweetest voice, "Mr Bloom, I'm sorry you had to see this, but perhaps it will give you an idea of the trouble I've been having. Ever since Mrs Howard arrived, there has been nothing but chaos. This silly Robyn creature is the worst!" he intoned with a heavy sigh.

"Well, Mr Stadnick," Mr Bloom said in a deceptively quiet voice, "this 'Robyn creature' is my daughter, and I asked her to work here, undercover, to find out why my hotel has been losing so much money." His eyebrows knit together, and his voice raised. "She called me yesterday evening and told me all about your little plot with a certain Coach Ratner to discredit Mrs Howard. What were you doing, Mr Stadnick, paying him to do your dirty work?"

"Lies, lies, I tell you!" Mr Stadnick spluttered in confusion. "I…"

"I really don't want to hear it," Mr Bloom said, in slow, measured tones. "Well, Mr Stadnick, despite your paltry attempts to blame your incompetence on everybody else, I think we all know what has really been going on around here. Shall we step into your – or should I say, Mrs Howard's – office and discuss it?"

As the two men left, one livid with anger, the other twittering nervously, the rest of the group burst into laughter.

"Wow!" Jim exclaimed. "It looks like a lot of people were willing to pay Mr Ratner to do a lot of rotten things, and it backfired on all of them! I knew that guy was a rat when he started shouting at you, Mum. In fact, that's why I followed him in the first place. Of course," Jim added humbly, "thanks to Robyn, you didn't really need my help after all."

"But *I* did," broke in Steve, "and I'd like to return the favour. So, what about it? How about letting me make a world-class skier out of you?"

So, Steve really did mean it. As Jim's parents thanked the champion for his generous offer, Jim got very quiet. A world-class skier, hmmm? Jim thought. Perhaps, someday. He already had the skis. Jim stroked his chin. He could just imagine it…

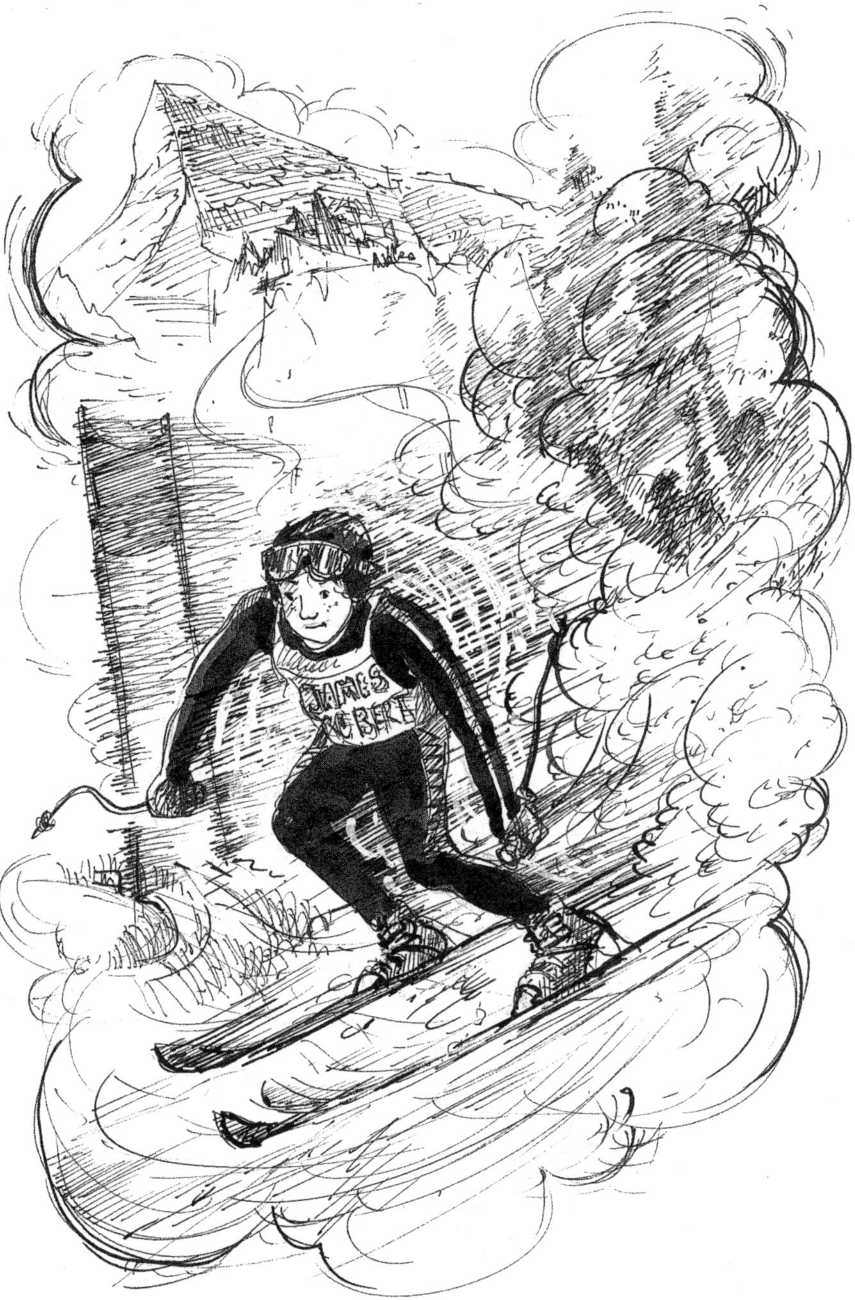
JAMES
ROBERT

From the Author

I have always loved adventure stories. Whenever I read them, I imagine myself as the main character, and I try to work out how I would cope with all of the exciting situations. James Robert Howard is like the person I wanted to be when I was young. He pretends to live other people's lives and, when a real adventure comes his way, his imagination and courage make him a hero.

Rebecca Weber

From the Illustrator

I grew up in England, where I developed an interest in art. I worked in ceramics for several years and taught at one of England's art institutes. In 1991, my family and I moved to Australia, where I got a job with the Australian Flying Arts School. I taught ceramics throughout Australia while logging more than 100,000 miles in a twin-engined plane. In 1995, we returned to England, where we now live.

Mike Spoor

CONFIDENCE AND COURAGE
Imagine this, James Robert
Follow That Spy!
Who Will Look Out for Danny?
Fuzz and the Glass Eye
Bald Eagles
Cottle Street

SOMETHING STRANGE
My Father the Mad Professor
A Theft in Time: Timedetectors II
CD and the Giant Cat
Chocolate!
White Elephants and Yellow Jackets
Dream Boat

ANOTHER TIME, ANOTHER PLACE
Cloudcatcher
Flags
The Dinosaur Connection
Myth or Mystery?
Where Did the Maya Go?
The Journal: Dear Future II

WHEN THINGS GO WRONG
The Long Walk Home
The Trouble with Patrick
The Kids from Quiller's Bend
Laughter is the Best Medicine
Wild Horses
The Sunday Horse

Written by **Rebecca Weber**
Illustrated by **Mike Spoor**
Edited by **David Nuss**
Designed by **Pat Madorin**

© 1997 Shortland Publications Inc.
All rights reserved.

05 04 03 02 01 00 99
11 10 9 8 7 6 5 4 3 2

Published by Shortland Publications Inc.

Distributed in New Zealand by Shortland Publications,
2B Cawley Street, Ellerslie, Auckland
Distributed in Australia by Rigby Heinemann,
a division of Reed International Books Australia Pty Ltd.
ACN 001 002 357, 22 Salmon Street, Port Melbourne, Victoria 3207
Distributed in the United Kingdom by Kingscourt Publishing Limited,
P.O. Box 1427, Freepost, London W6 9BR

Printed by Colorcraft, Hong Kong
ISBN: 1-57257-677-4